FIGURES IN CHINA'S SPACE INDUSTRY

Who is Lu Shijia?

www.royalcollins.com

FIGURES IN CHINA'S SPACE INDUSTRY

Who is Lu Shijia?

By Ye Qiang and Dong Pingping

Books Beyond Boundaries

ROYAL COLLINS

In the spring of 1926, thousands of students and citizens in Beijing took to the street in protest against the Japanese army's request to "remove national defense facilities at Dagukou." Subsequently, the March 18 Massacre occurred. The tragic incident greatly touched the 15-year-old Lu Xiuzhen. When she saw in the newspaper that many female martyrs had the character "shi" (meaning man, scholar, or soldier) in their names, she suddenly decided to have this character in her name too. Then, she added the character "jia" (excellent) to the end, making her name "Shijia." Young Lu Shijia thought to herself: "I will be a better person than all of them."

Around 1935, Lu Shijia and her fiancé Zhang Wei decided to study abroad. At that time, China was suffering in wars, and foreign forces frequently occupied her territory. Lu Shijia realized that building planes was much more urgent than studying stars. Therefore, she gave up on her interest in astronomy and went to Germany to study aviation.

Another important reason that attracted her to this field was the opportunity to study with Dr. Ludwig Prandtl, the world-renowned scholar and founder of modern fluid mechanics.

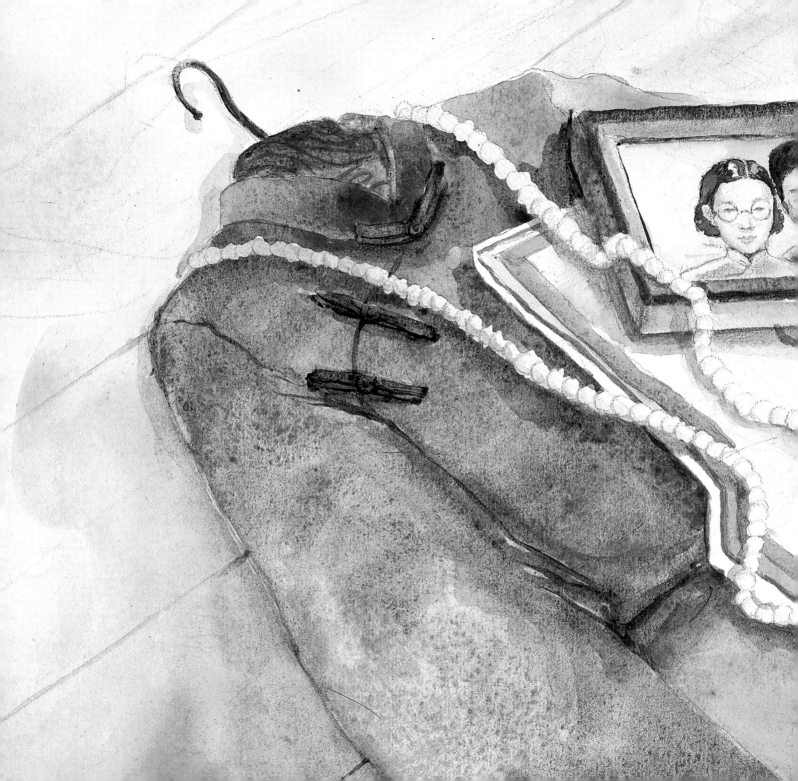

Fearing the uncertainties she would face in a troubled and chaotic time, Lu Shijia's family insisted that she be engaged before she left. In addition to exchanging rings at the engagement ceremony, Lu Shijia solemnly gave Zhang Wei a pen with the words "do not forget our homeland" engraved by her own hand.

Lu Shijia arrived at Göttingen University in Germany in 1938, hoping to study fluid mechanics with Prandtl. She did not meet the professor during her first two visits to the university, either because of an inconvenient time or because the professor was out. On her third visit, she finally made an appointment through the professor's secretary.

Prandtl has never accepted female graduate students, let alone students from such "backward" countries as China at the time. He thus rejected Lu's request, saying that he had publicly announced that he would no longer be taking on students. He believed that it was simply impossible for this small Eastern girl to be his graduate student – fluid mechanics is a subject that requires prodigious mathematical skill!

Lu understood the professor's implication. She enthusiastically told him about her love for China and her determination to make her country become a better place. Prandtl was touched but said it would be too difficult for her to take his class. Lu Shijia said, "You can test me. If I can't pass your test, I won't bother you anymore." Finally, Prandtl agreed to give her a test in two months' time.

Two months later, Lu Shijia came again as promised. Prandtl wanted to "scare her off" with some tough questions, but Lu tackled all of them quickly. Although all questions on the test were exceptionally hard, Lu received an excellent grade.

Amazed by Lu's talent, Prandtl kept his promise and accepted her as his last advisee. Lu thus became Prandtl's only Asian female graduate student.

Dr. Prandtl was an upright intellectual against Nazism. He was moved by Lu Shijia's devotion to her country and her persistent research spirit. The teacher and student maintained a good friendship in the following decades.

Lu Shijia studied at Göttingen University during World War II. The university restricted the Chinese students from using experimental facilities and kept the experimental technology strictly confidential. These limitations made Lu's learning very difficult, given the poor living conditions.

Nevertheless, Lu Shijia was not distressed by the setbacks. She used rigorous theoretical methods to deal with a complex hydrodynamic problem and attained the results in complete agreement with those of the university's Aerodynamic Research Institute. At the beginning of 1942, Lu completed her thesis "The Upward Roll of the Cylindrical Jet When It Meets Vertical Airflow" and obtained her doctorate.

After graduation, she first worked as a teaching assistant at the Berlin Institute of Technology and then as a research engineer in the Saxonburg Shipyard's Berlin Design and Research Department. In early 1944, she was forced to leave her job because the bombing destroyed the department. Later, she returned to Göttingen University on the recommendation of her mentor, Prandtl. However, it was not a fruitful opportunity either.

At the time, the head of the Aerodynamics Institute of Göttingen University was a member of the Nazi Party. He refused to have Lu Shijia work in the institute because of her firm condemnation of the aggressive acts of Japanese imperialism. Lu could only work on the subjects assigned to her in a separate room. However, she still discovered Nazi research results about aircraft flying into water and made changes to some important data. She said: "Although I can't go to the front to fight the fascists, I can at least try to make them kill fewer people."

Her strong national pride made her resign in anger, and she decided to return to the motherland as soon as possible. At the end of 1945, Zhang Wei, Lu Shijia, and their three-year-old daughter set off from Germany. They first arrived in Switzerland and stayed there for a year because of the war. Later, at the suggestion of their friends, they boarded a ship from Marseille, France. From there, they crossed the Mediterranean, set out to the Atlantic Ocean, circled around the Cape of Good Hope, crossed the Indian Ocean, and landed in Saigon, Vietnam. After that, they continued their journey to Hong Kong and finally returned home.

In 1952, the Chinese government decided to build a new type of aviation university – the Beijing Institute of Technology (now the Beihang University). Lu Shijia was on the preparatory committee, and she actively taught aerodynamics and other courses at the institute after it was established. In a lecture on Magnetohydrodynamics, she proposed an incisive theory: "The essence of fluid is vortex. Fluid can't stand rubbing. It will give out vortex once it is rubbed." Many hydrodynamics works quoted her theory afterwards. She also led young teachers of the institute to write the earliest academic works and teaching materials on relevant disciplines in China, such as *High-Speed Viscous Fluid Mechanics*, *Electromagnetohydrodynamics*, *Hypersonic Regime*, etc. They built the first water tank at the Beijing Institute of Technology and a wind tunnel ...

"I know that it often takes several generations to achieve a significant research results. The scientists' responsibility is to explore. I always hope that China will make a breakthrough in aviation science and technology. I want to be a paving stone and do some exploration work that future generations can build upon."

Lu's dream came true. She was a pioneer and a bright star in the history of China's aerospace development.

25

About the Authors

Ye Qiang studied oil paintings at Sichuan Fine Arts Institute. After graduating in 2001, he began teaching as an associate professor in the department of New Media Art and Design at Beihang University. Ye's paintings have been displayed in hundreds of national and international exhibitions, and he has held solo exhibitions in galleries, including the Shanghai Art Museum, several times. Ye's paintings and scholarship can be found in more than 20 academic journals and monographs. He has also published seven textbooks.

Dong Pingping is Vice-Secretary of the Party Committee and a member of the Supervisory Commission of the department of New Media Art and Design at Beijing University of Aeronautics and Astronautics.

Figures in China's Space Industry:
Who is Lu Shijia?

Written by Ye Qiang and Dong Pingping

First published in 2023 by Royal Collins Publishing Group Inc.
Groupe Publication Royal Collins Inc.
BKM Royalcollins Publishers Private Limited

Headquarters: 550-555 boul. René-Lévesque O Montréal (Québec) H2Z1B1 Canada
India office: 805 Hemkunt House, 8th Floor, Rajendra Place, New Delhi 110 008

Original Edition © Shaanxi People's Education Press Co., Ltd.

ISBN: 978-1-4878-1108-2

To find out more about our publications, please visit www.royalcollins.com.